D1061462

GIANT VEHICLES

An Imagination Library Series

GIANT LOADERS

Jim Mezzanotte

GARETH**STEVENS**
GS
PUBLISHING

A Member of the WRC Media Family of Companies

Please visit our web site at: www.garethstevens.com
For a free color catalog describing Gareth Stevens Publishing's list of high-quality books and multimedia programs, call 1-800-542-2595 (USA) or 1-800-387-3178 (Canada). Gareth Stevens Publishing's fax: (414) 332-3567.

Library of Congress Cataloging-in-Publication Data

Mezzanotte, Jim.
    Giant loaders / by Jim Mezzanotte.
        p. cm. – (Giant vehicles)
    Includes bibliographical references and index.
    ISBN 0-8368-4913-2 (lib. bdg.)
    ISBN 0-8368-4920-5 (softcover)
    1. Earthmoving machinery–Juvenile literature. 2. Loaders (Machines)–Juvenile literature. I. Title.
    TA725.M42   2005
    621.8'65–dc22   2005045155

First published in 2006 by
Gareth Stevens Publishing
A Member of the WRC Media Family of Companies
330 West Olive Street, Suite 100
Milwaukee, WI 53212 USA

Editorial direction: Mark J. Sachner
Editor: JoAnn Early Macken
Art direction: Tammy West
Cover design and page layout: Kami M. Koenig
Photo editor: Diane Laska-Swanke
Picture researcher: Martin Levick

Photo credits: Cover, Courtesy of Komatsu America Corp.; pp. 5, 7, 9, 11, 13, 15, 17, 19, 21 © Eric Orlemann

This edition copyright © 2006 by Gareth Stevens, Inc. All rights reserved to Gareth Stevens, Inc. No part of this book may be reproduced, stored in a retrieval system, or transmitted in any form or by any means, electronic, mechanical, photocopying, recording, or otherwise, without the prior written permission of the publisher except for the inclusion of brief quotations in an acknowledged review.

Printed in the United States of America

1 2 3 4 5 6 7 8 9 09 08 07 06 05

COVER: This giant loader can carry huge amounts of dirt and rock. It was made by the Komatsu company.

Table of Contents

A Big Load

Giant loaders move huge amounts of stuff. They mostly work in **mines**. They move dirt and rock. They also move **coal**, gold, and silver. They put their loads into giant dump trucks. A giant loader has a big **bucket** in front to dig and carry loads.

These loaders have giant wheels for good **traction**. They have powerful engines. They are tough and reliable. At mines, work never stops. The machines work every day of the year. They work at night, too. They work in rain and snow, cold and heat. The loaders have to be quick. As soon as a loader dumps one load, it goes back for another.

The Caterpillar company made this giant loader. It is working at a mine. With its big bucket, it will move this pile of rocks in no time!

Bigger and Better

The first loaders were used in the 1920s. They were regular **tractors**. People put buckets on the front for loading. By the 1940s, companies made special machines. They were built just to be loaders.

The loaders got more powerful. They could dig and not just carry. They got bigger, too. A big loader does a job faster. By the 1970s, there were many giant loaders.

Today, loaders work in mines all over the world. They do many jobs. In some places, they have replaced large diggers. They dig just as well. But they move much quicker.

In the 1970s, this Michigan 675 was the world's largest loader. But it is small compared to the biggest loaders made today!

Big Wheels

Some loaders have **tracks** instead of wheels. But giant loaders have wheels. They are called wheel loaders.

Giant wheel loaders are heavy. Their wheels have to be large and strong. The wheels are taller than cars and trucks. They are more than twice as tall as an adult. A wheel weighs many times more than a car. One tire costs as much as a car!

How do you steer these loaders? They actually bend in the middle! The front and back are attached by a hinge. The whole front turns.

You would not want a flat tire with this loader! You cannot steer the huge front wheels. When you steer, the whole front turns right or left.

How Big Is Big?

Giant loaders are massive machines. They have frames made of thick steel. The arms that lift the bucket are thick steel, too. The arms have to lift big buckets high in the air. These loaders are tall. They can be as tall as a two-story building. They have ladders to reach the cab.

LeTourneau is a U.S. company. Today, it makes the biggest loader in the world. This loader is called the L-2350. It weighs more than a half million pounds (227,000 kilograms).

It has a huge bucket. You could park a car inside it! The bucket can carry fifty times the weight of a small car.

This loader is the LeTourneau L-2350. It is the world's largest loader. It will fill a giant dump truck in just a few trips. A ladder folds down so you can climb aboard.

Big Power

Loader engines are huge. Most car engines have four or six **cylinders**. Some loader engines have sixteen cylinders. Loaders have **diesel** engines. They use diesel **fuel**, not gasoline. The engines can produce 2,000 **horsepower** — over ten times more than many car engines. Loaders have their engines in back. Nothing blocks the view in front.

LeTourneau loaders use electric power. Each wheel has its own electric motor. The diesel engine turns a generator that makes electric power for these motors.

Hydraulic cylinders lift the bucket. A cylinder is a big tube. Inside, it has a smaller tube called a piston. The cylinder has oil in it. Machines force the oil up the inside of the cylinder. The oil pushes the piston. The piston slides up. The cylinder grows longer. It lifts the bucket!

A Komatsu loader fills a giant dump truck. You can see a shiny piston above the front wheel. This loader has a huge, powerful engine in back.

In the Cab

People in loaders work long hours. They work in all kinds of weather. But they stay comfortable in the cab. The cab keeps out noise and dust. It has a heater. It has air-conditioning. There is even a stereo!

Today, many loaders have **joy sticks**, not steering wheels. You may have used a joy stick to play a video game. Joy sticks are used to steer loaders. On some loaders, joy sticks move the bucket, too.

The cab has **gauges**, lights, and buzzers. They tell if something is wrong. The cab has a computer screen, too. It gives information about the loader and the work it is doing.

Here is the cab of a LeTourneau L-2350. You sit in a big, comfortable seat. You steer and move the bucket with the two joy sticks. A computer screen is straight ahead.

Loaders at Work

Most giant loaders work in pit mines. A pit mine is a huge hole. Machines dig up the earth. Then they dig for coal, gold, and silver deep in the ground.

At mines, giant loaders do many jobs. Loaders dig. Their buckets have teeth for digging. Sometimes, loaders help large diggers with a job. Other times, loaders do all the digging. Loaders also help take things away. They drop big loads in dump trucks. The loaders fill giant trucks very quickly.

This loader is working in a gold mine. The loader is in a deep hole.

Loader Makers

LeTourneau is famous for its giant loaders. It makes many different sizes, including the world's biggest. LeTourneau loaders have many **innovations**. Caterpillar and Komatsu also make giant loaders. These companies also make other big machines, such as bulldozers and trucks.

Customers choose the loader they want. They choose tires. They may choose engines. They choose buckets. There are different buckets for different jobs. **Engineers** use computers to **design** and test the loaders.

How do loaders get to mines? They are too big for trucks, trains, or ships. They travel in pieces. At a mine, they are put together. They are expensive. A single giant loader can cost more than four million dollars.

These men are helping to build a new LeTourneau loader. You can see part of the huge engine. The rear wheel is not done yet. An electric motor will turn it.

Let's Load!

It takes a lot of skill to run a giant loader. There is a lot to do. One hand steers. The other hand controls the bucket. The bucket moves up and down. It also "curls." Curling up holds a load. Curling down drops it.

Safety is important. You have to watch for people and other machines. But you have to work fast. You put the bucket down and scoop up a load. You head to the dump truck. Keep the bucket low so you do not tip over! Drop your load and turn around. Start over again!

Operating this Komatsu loader is a hard job. You have to drop each load in the right spot. The loads are huge and heavy. You have to be careful—and quick!

More to Read and View

Books

C is for Construction: Big Trucks and Diggers from A to Z. Caterpillar (Chronicle Books)

Earth Movers. Mighty Movers (series). Sarah Tieck (Buddy Books)

If I Could Drive a Loader. Michael Teitelbaum (Cartwheel)

Road Builders. B. G. Hennessy (Viking)

Wheel Loaders. Earth Movers (series). Joanne Randolph (PowerKids Press)

DVDs and Videos

At Work With Heavy Equipment (Tony Nassour)

I Love Big Machines (Consumervision)

I Love Cat Machines (Tapeworm)

Modern Marvels: More Earthmovers (A&E Home Video)

Web Sites

Web sites change frequently, but we believe the following web sites are going to last. You can also use good search engines, such as **Yahooligans**! (www.yahooligans.com) or **Google** (www.google.com) to find more information about giant vehicles. Some keywords that will help you are *bucket loader, loader, wheel loader, Caterpillar, Komatsu,* and *LeTourneau*.

auto.howstuffworks.com/diesel1.htm
This web site shows how a diesel engine works.

science.howstuffworks.com/ hydraulic.htm
Visit this web site to learn more about how hydraulic machines work.

www.cat.com/cda/layout?m= 37840&x=7&location=drop
At this web site, you can see many different Caterpillar machines, including giant wheel loaders. Choose "wheel loaders." Then choose a model by clicking on the model number. You can make the pictures larger. Click on "Benefits & Features" to see more.

www.komatsuamerica.com/index. cfm?resource_id=9
The Komatsu web site has many wheel loaders. Click "wheel loaders" and then click "specs" to see a picture of each one.

www.letourneau-inc.com/html/ equipment/mining/mining.html
Visit this web site and click the model numbers to see pictures of many LeTourneau wheel loaders, including the world's largest loader, the L-2350. You can also learn more about joy sticks.

Glossary

You can find these words on the pages listed. Reading a word in a sentence helps you to understand it even better.

bucket (BUK-it): on a loader, the metal container in front used to dig and carry loads. 4, 6, 10, 12, 14, 16, 18, 20

coal (KOLE): a black material made of long-dead plants. Coal is a fuel, and it is often used at electric power plants. 4, 16

cylinders (SIL-in-durz): tubes inside an engine where fuel explodes, giving the engine power. 12

design (dee-ZINE): make a plan for building something. 18

diesel (DEE-zull): the name for a kind of engine and the special fuel it uses. Most diesel engines are very reliable. They often use less fuel than gas engines. 12

engineers (en-jun-EARZ): people who design machines. 18

fuel (FYULE): something that burns to provide energy. 12

gauges (GAY-jez): devices that measure something, such as temperature. 14

horsepower (HORS-pow-ur): the amount of power an engine makes, based on how much work one horse can do. 12

hydraulic (hi-DRAW-lick): having to do with using water or another liquid to move something. 12

innovations (in-oh-VAY-shunz): new inventions or ways of doing things. 18

joy sticks (JOY stiks): levers that move forward and back and from side to side to control a machine. 14

mines (MINES): places where coal, gold, silver, and other things are taken out of the ground. Some mines are underground tunnels. Other mines are big holes, or pits. 4

tracks (TRAX): belts that circle around a row of wheels to move a machine. One wheel in each belt makes it turn. Some tracks are metal plates linked together. Other tracks are loops made of rubber. 8

traction (TRAK-shun): the grip that something has on a surface. To dig and carry heavy loads, a giant loader needs a good grip on the ground. 4

tractors (TRAK-turz): vehicles that pull things, such as trailers or equipment. 6

Index